KODANSHA LIBRARY OF JAPANESE ART

No. 5

Plate 2. WOMAN CHANGING CLOTHES. *Painted in color on silk. Ca. 1798. Collection of Mrs. Sue Hara.*

喜多川歌麿

KITAGAWA UTAMARO

(1753—1806)

Text by
ICHITARO KONDO

English adaptation by
CHARLES S. TERRY

CHARLES E. TUTTLE COMPANY
Rutland, Vermont—Tokyo, Japan

NOTE ON THE ENGLISH TEXT

It has been a privilege to work with Mr. Kondo's scholarly and enlightening text. In reading it, I found myself wondering how he managed to put so much information in such a tiny space. Unfortunately, I found that I was unable to match him in this respect. He was writing for Japanese readers, and since one of the main purposes of this series is to reach Westerners who do not possess a detailed knowledge of Japan, I found it necessary to amplify and abbreviate considerably. Mr. Kondo, of course, is not responsible for my changes.

Old Japanese names are given in the Japanese style— surname first—and modern names in the Western style.

C. S. T.

Published by the Charles E. Tuttle Company, of Rutland, Vermont & Tokyo, Japan, by arrangement with Kodansha, Tokyo. All rights reserved by Kodansha, without whose written permission no part of the contents of this book may be reproduced.

First English edition, March, 1956

Fourth printing, 1959

Library of Congress Catalog Card No. 56 8490

Printed in Japan by
Kyodo Printing Co., Ltd., Tokyo

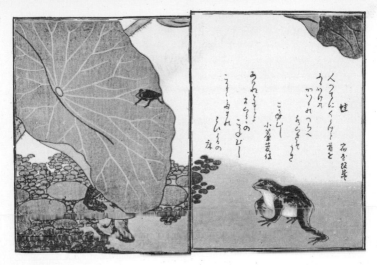

Plate 3. From "A Collection of Insects."
Color print. 1788.

UTAMARO

The ukiyo-e was an art of the lower classes, and in the hierarchical society of the Tokugawa period it was hardly regarded as an art at all by those who counted. The men who designed ukiyo-e prints were considered mere artisans, and facts about their lives were only vaguely known even while they were still living. Utamaro is regarded today as the greatest of them all, but scholars are still uncertain where he was born and whether he was married or not. Edo, Osaka, Kyoto, and Kawagoe have all been suggested as his birthplace, but for a variety of reasons it appears altogether more likely that he was born in some country village. In any case, he came to Edo in his youth and began to study painting under Toriyama Sekien. The latter, a disciple of Kano Gyokuen, was a lover of poetry and light verse, as well as the designer of many picture albums. The rollicking life of the Edo demimonde was his element, and he counted among his friends many happy-go-lucky actors, playwrights, and men about town. Through him Utamaro had frequent chances to meet such people, and the friendships that he formed with them led him to design many illustrations for the farcical poems that they so enjoyed composing.

Sekien also used the name Toyofusa, and at first Utamaro called himself Hosho, using the first character for Toyofusa, also pronounced *ho*. His earliest known work bearing this signature is dated 1775. It is the illustrated text of a play, and most of his other early works appear to have had some connection with the theater. They show the strong influence of Katsukawa Shunsho, who was at the time a leading painter of actors.

Through Sekien and his friends Utamaro eventually gained an introduction to Tsutaya Juzaburo, the most brilliant and affluent publisher of prints in Edo. Known for short as Tsutaju, this remarkable man was a noted lover of the theater, a composer of good light poetry, and a guardian angel for struggling print designers. As he had often done for others, he took Utamaro under his wing and provided him with food and shelter. Utamaro actually moved into Tsutaya's house in 1783 or 1784, and it was at this time that his real work as an artist began. After only a few years under Tsutaya's protection, he gained a place alongside Shunsho, Torii Kiyonaga, Kitao Shigemasa, and the other famous ukiyo-e artists of the day.

By this time he had changed his name to Utamaro and had begun to specialize in pictures of beautiful women. The earlier ones were more or less obsequious imitations of Shigemasa and, especially, Kiyonaga. During the 1780's Kiyonaga's limpid beauties made him the most popular of all the artists. His subjects were usually tall, healthy-looking women, and they had considerable appeal

Plate 4. From "The Charms of Prostitutes
in the Four Seasons." Color print. 1784 or 1785.

in themselves, but the real charm of his works lay in the dazzling colors of the clothing and incidentals rather than in the faces and figures. Utamaro designed dozens of prints in Kiyonaga's style during these formative years. It should not be forgotten, however, that he also painted a number of albums of a very different type, pictures of birds, fish, and insects, executed in very accurate detail and revealing a strong desire on the artist's part to draw closer to nature than was possible in Kiyonaga's medium (see Plate 3). The years 1787 and 1788 were devoted to works of these two types, but, by synthesizing the two approaches involved, Utamaro was gradually developing a new style of his own. In 1788 Sekien died, but by this time his pupil was ready to proceed on his own. In 1789 he felt confident enough to stamp one of his prints with a seal that might loosely be interpreted to mean "I have arrived."

The year 1790 was pivotal for Utamaro in several respects. In the fifth moon of the year the government instituted a Confucianist reform and among other things attempted to curb the publication of ukiyo-e, which it regarded as conducive to frivolity and immorality. In the eighth moon a woman very closely connected with the artist died. It is not known whether she was his mother, his wife, or his child, but she was evidently quite important to him. From this time on he began to publish only pictures of women in a new style he had discovered.

Unlike his predecessors, he concentrated on the sheer physical beauty of his subjects. Instead of the customary full-length view, he often showed only the upper part of the body. The clothing was plain in comparison with that of Kiyonaga's beauties, and the background usually consisted merely of a solid color or a gleaming surface of powdered mica. The emphasis was on color values rather than line, and the effect was one of softness and warmth. In some cases the artist used almost no contour lines, as

青
楼
尓
和
嘉
廣
嶋
踊
語

京
町
二
丁
目

角
町
丁
目

き
よ
ゑ

せ
き
や

た
と

哥
麿
画

*Plate 5. From "Niwaka Celebration in a House of
Prostitution." Color print. 1784 or 1785. See Plate 11.*

for example in *New Brocade Design in the Utamaro Style* (Plate 39) and in the faces in *A Woman's Day* (Plate 20). His new approach enabled him to bring out the full beauty of a woman's skin and facial features, and for this reason his beauties are the loveliest of all.

One important thing about Utamaro's women is that they represent not particular individuals, but the artist's ideal of feminine beauty. They vary to some extent in age and social status, but whether middle-aged housewife or youthful prostitute, they have the same voluptuous bodies and beautiful faces. There is irony in this. Utamaro himself was a very ugly man. A picture of him painted a few years after his death (Plate 46) shows him to have been fat, flabby, and rather dissipated in appearance. Presumably this was how he looked just before he died, and he may possibly have been more handsome in his youth, but his loveliest women were painted only thirteen years before he sank to the condition in which we see him here. His story then is the ancient tragedy of a homely old man in search of a beautiful woman to love him. The tall handsome youth seen in several of his late prints represents his ideal of himself.

A number of critics have read a different meaning into Utamaro's work. Comparing the svelte, sensuous beauties that came from his brush with the degenerate face in his own portrait, they have come to the conclusion that his prints were the product of a diseased and lascivious mind. Speaking of an Utamaro creation, Arthur Ficke, for instance, said: "In the slender delicacy of this figure, the splendid black of her elaborate coiffure, the sensuous grace and refinement, the languor and exhaustion—in all these speak the supersensible gropings and hungers of Utamaro. Out of a living woman he created his disturbing symbol of the impossible desires that are no less subtle or painful because they are born of the flesh. With nerves keyed beyond the healthy pitch, he dreamed this melody whose

Plate 6. THE SILHOUETTE BEAUTY *or* WOMEN OF
THE NAKATA HOUSE. *Color print. Ca. 1794.*

strange minor chords could stir the satiated spirit. He caught and idealized the lines and colors of mortal weariness."

Is there any real basis for this conclusion? Utamaro lived in the gay quarters of old Edo and associated continually with entertainers, waitresses, prostitutes, and their patrons. His surroundings were hardly what one would describe as edifying, but they were the same surroundings that produced Kiyonaga, Sharaku, and the other great ukiyo-e artists, none of whom have been especially criticized on this score. Furthermore, the impression the life of Edo during this age gives a modern student is not one of "mortal weariness," but of immortal boisterousness. Utamaro had a healthy love of nature, expressed in his lifelike animal pictures, and he often painted on such worthy themes as motherly love and feminine virtue. There is no real evidence that his nerves were "keyed beyond a healthy pitch," and this judgment must be regarded as purely subjective. An aging man, favored with neither a dashing figure nor a handsome face, he may well have conceived of young women as more beautiful, graceful, tender, and desirable than they frequently are, but one need not search for ugly reasons for this. Sad though it may be, it is certainly not, in itself, evil.

Though Utamaro may have been discontent with his age and looks, he had no reason to be dissatisfied with his triumph as an artist. His prints were known all over Japan and even in China. Publishers fought to buy his designs. Up to 1793 he worked only for a few big publishers, such as Tsutaya Juzaburo and Tsuruya Kiemon, but afterward he designed for more than forty different houses. Like certain other print artists who attained great popularity, however, he began to draw too much to maintain his old standards. Art ceased to be a passion for him, and the quality of his paintings declined greatly. The faces of his women became hard and lifeless. Gone

Plate 7. THE VULGAR ONES.
From "Manners and Customs on Three Levels."
Color print. 1795 or 1796.

Plate 8. LOVE IN CONTEMPLATION. *Detail of Plate 1 (cover)*.

was their freshness, their youth, their soft, inviting flesh.

The change in Utamaro's art reflected also a change in his temperament, for he himself by no means grew old gracefully. Popularity and honor went to his head. He made calumnious statements about the many artists who imitated him, accused his publishers of being skinflints for buying their designs instead of his alone, and boasted that no one could imitate his style. Ignoring the days when he himself had drawn pictures of actors, he proclaimed that he was too good to waste his time on a bunch of hams, that Sharaku and Toyokuni had done so only because they were inferior to him. A good deal of this talk must have stemmed from wounded vanity. In Utamaro's last years, the world was changing. The youthful Toyokuni had already gained a measure of popularity, and Hokusai was arriving on the scene with his new landscape prints, which were to become the most popular of all in the next generation. Utamaro could hardly have failed to observe that he was losing his dominant position to others. His braggadocio was no more than a support for his confidence in himself. In his late pictures he became a handsome young swain, but in reality he was a crotchety old nuisance. There is the same pathetic protest in his boasting as in his longing for youth and beauty and love.

In 1804, Utamaro published a set of prints which showed the great military hero Hideyoshi amusing himself with his five concubines (see Plates 43–45), and this greatly offended the Tokugawa government, which considered the work an indirect gibe against it. The artist was thrown into prison for a short time, and his hands were bound in chains for fifty days. This was the final blow to his pride. Defeated and rejected, he gave up his battle against the trends of the age. He had nothing more to live for, and in 1806 he died. His death was tragic, but his vision of beauty was undying. In modern times he has recovered the fame he tried so desperately to keep from losing.

Plate 9. KINTARO AND YAMAUBA. *Ca. 1798.*

Plate 10

THE HERON GIRL

*From "A Collection of Contemporary Dancers."   Color print.
Tokyo National Museum.*

The print reproduced here is from an album made around
1791 and containing pictures of women performing famous
dances. Three or four other prints from the same series
are known to exist.

"The Heron Girl" is the story of a beautiful young
woman who was about to be married, but was slain by a
rejected suitor. Her departed spirit, it is said, became a
beautiful white heron. In the Kabuki-stage version of the
dance, the performer enters clad in a white outer robe,
but at one point this is suddenly removed, revealing a
colorful kimono underneath, like the one worn by the
girl here.

Utamaro's interest is focused not on the clothing, as
was often the case with other artists, but on the girl's face,
and only parts of the headdress and kimono are shown.
The background, made of ground muscovite, glimmers
softly. Utamaro often used glints of this sort to set off
the soft beauty of a woman's skin.

Large facial portraits were first introduced to the art of
ukiyo-e by Katsukawa Shunsho in the 1760's, but Shunsho
and other artists before Utamaro employed the form only
for actors, and Utamaro was the first to use it in painting
beautiful women.

During the Edo period the women of the famous red-light district in Yoshiwara held an annual celebration called a *niwaka*, on which occasion they got themselves up as men and performed farces or other comical skits for their own amusement. The names of four women are mentioned in the title of this print, but only two are shown. They are wearing elàborate costumes intended for male Kabuki roles. The fine, intricate lines and profuse coloring are unusual for Utamaro, but despite the detailed attention to clothing, the print has a touch of the artist's characteristic simplicity, and the faces reveal his proclivity for portraying the physical beauty of women. The picture probably dates from 1784 or 1785, when the artist was still imitating Shunsho and Kiyonaga, and it bears many traits common to their works. Three other sheets that appear to belong to the same set still exist today.

Plate 12. NEEDLEWORK. *Detail of Plate 17.*

Plate 13. Needlework. *Detail of Plate 17.*

Plate 14

THE FICKLE TYPE

From "Ten Physiognomical Studies of Women." Color print with mica background. Tokyo National Museum.

The name of this print seems appropriate to the amorous deviltry in the woman's eyes. She looks as though she has just spotted a man whose attention she would like to attract.

The portrait is a classic Utamaro, having all the main features of the style he created around 1790. Attention is centered entirely on the woman's physical beauty. The clothing is unobtrusive, and the background consists merely of a mica finish, which suggests the tinted light of early evening. Throughout the lines are brief, and emphasis is primarily on subtle color values.

The inscription at the upper left says that the series to which the work belongs is composed of ten prints, but at present only five others are known. Utamaro appears to have left the set incomplete, but it is probably connected with the series to which the next plate belongs.

This famous print is another example of Utamaro's style at its best. The woman being somewhat older than the one shown on the preceding page, her eyebrows have been shaved, after the custom among matrons of the past.

The name of the set from which the picture is taken mentions ten prints, but only four are known to exist or to have existed, and one of these is the same as a picture in *Ten Physiognomical Studies of Women* (Plate 14). Altogether, then, there are ten prints in the two series. Presumably, Utamaro started one, stopped work on it for some reason, and returned to it later, changing the title at the time. All the prints are in the same style, but tho *Physiognomical Studies* appear to be earlier than the *Physiognomical Types*.

Plate 16

Love Requited

From "A Selection of Poems, Section on Love." Color print with mica background. Tokyo National Museum.

To judge from the title, Utamaro based this album on an ancient anthology of poems, but he portrayed his subjects very much in the style of his own day. Apparently only four other prints from the series still exist, but it seems likely that there was originally one for each of the six most famous poets of the Heian period. The other known prints are entitled "Love in Contemplation," "Long-Suffering Love," and "Love Appearing." The women shown in these are older than those in other Utamaro albums. The background of this print is an example of the rare mixture of mica and red pigment.

Plate 17

NEEDLEWORK

Three color prints joined. Tokyo National Museum. See Plates 12 & 13 for details.

Utamaro's favorite subjects were women of pleasure, waitresses, and other undomestic types, but occasionally he painted housewives busy at their chores. This said, we hasten to add that they were still the same women, with only the costumes and settings changed. The lady in the center of this nicely composed group is intended to be fairly old, for her eyebrows have been shaved, and her obi is tied in front in the old fashion of women getting on in years. Still she has the same facial features and soft skin as the younger woman examining a strip of black cloth on the left (see details in Plates 12 and 13).

As Edmond de Goncourt has pointed out, Japanese women are "petite, petite, petite et rondelette," but in Utamaro's dream they become tall, slender goddesses. Some critics have found dire and lascivious implications in this. They seem to regard Utamaro's willowy beauties as the product of a perverted passion. James Michener, in *The Floating World*, has given a brilliant answer to this argument, and there is little reason for going into the matter further, but certainly this print is a rebuttal in itself. One hesitates to imagine how tall these women would be if they stood up, but it would take a fairly prejudiced critic to conclude that the picture represents anything harmful or even odd. After all the kind of women one likes is no more than a matter of taste. Utamaro obviously liked them tall, but that is not very unusual.

Plates 18 & 19

THE HOUR OF THE DOG

From "A Day in a House of Prostitution." Color print. Collection of Mr. Sei-ichiro Takahashi.

In pre-modern times the Japanese divided the day into twelve two-hour periods, which were named for animals, and this album contains a print for each of these. The artist dealt only with the private activities of the prostitutes, and no patrons are shown. The hour of the dog, which ran from eight to ten in the evening, is represented by this picture of a woman writing a letter as she awaits a customer. The young girl to whom she is whispering is a serving girl destined to become a prostitute when she grows older.

One can recognize incipient formalism here. The body and face of the woman are far less real than in Utamaro's earlier portraits (see Plates 14–16), and the bulge representing her leg is entirely false. Still the facial expressions are lively, and the eyes are exceedingly vivid.

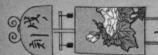

Plate 20

THE HOUR OF THE HORSE

From "A Woman's Day." Color print. Collection of Mr. Sei-ichiro Takahashi.

Like the album from which the previous plate was taken, *A Woman's Day* was presumably composed of twelve prints, one for each of the ancient divisions of the day, but only those for the hours between eight in the morning and six in the evening, five prints in all, are known today. Whether Utamaro completed the set or not is uncertain.

There is a statement on the print saying that "in ancient times women entered the bath during the hour of the monkey." That would have been between four and six in the evening. Apparently by Utamato's day women had begun to bathe earlier, since the hour of the horse, at which time the women are shown here emerging from the bath, lasted from noon to two o'clock.

The figures of the two women are nicely balanced, and the mild yellow of the background provides a fine contrast to the sienna and indigo of the standing woman's kimono. Utamaro frequently economized on lines, and in this print he gave the faces no contours at all. Presumably he was trying to bring out the softness and whiteness of the women's skin. The technique was original with him.

This album appears to have been printed around 1792.

娘日時計　午ノ刻

古代者女湯以甲刻
當此歟。

歌麿筆

Plate 21

HANA OF THE OGIYA

*From "The Most Beautiful Women of the Day."   Color print.
Collection of Mr. Sei-ichiro Takahashi.*

Utamaro painted the collection of famous geisha from
which this plate is taken some time around 1794. The
album includes eleven women, but two of them are shown
together, so that there are only ten prints in all. The
portraits have the elements of idealism ordinarily found in
the artist's work, but one gets the feeling that he was
trying to make these women as delectable as possible.
Hana, the coquette shown here, worked in an establishment
named the Ogiya and was one of the most famous courtesans
of her day. Seated here in a careless pose, as was often
the case with Utamaro's women, she is smoothing her hair
with one of the long metal hairpins that serve to decorate
Japanese wamen's elaborate headdresses, while holding a
Japanese pipe in her other hand. The device of putting
the subject on one side and leaving the other blank is an
interesting compositional innovation.

Plates 22, 23 & 24

Diving Women

Set of three color prints. Tokyo National Museum.

The women of many Japanese fishing communities earn money by diving in the shore waters for various marine products, in this case abalone. Ukiyo-e pictures of these hardy divers are rather numerous, but none excels this, which is among Utamaro's most highly appreciated works. As a rule Japanese painters are rather poor at nudes. They always seem to introduce odd designs into the human body. There is a certain lack of faithfulness here too, but the failure is not too pronounced, and the women have a strong sensual appeal. The middle section resembles Utamaro's many pictures based on a fairy tale about a little strong boy named Kintaro and a wild woman of the hills, Yamauba, who brought him up. Utamaro painted this pair often in the late 1790's.

The composition of this triptych is loosely in the form of an isosceles triangle and for this reason is exceedingly stable.

Plate 22

Plate 23. See preceding plate.

Plate 24. See preceding plate.

Utamaro designed many prints on the theme of maternal love, and this is one of the most charming. The rather disheveled young mother creates an impression of ease and grace as she works away at the peach, and the waving feet of the serious-faced little boy show that the artist was no stranger to children. The colors are as fresh and delicious as the fruit itself. There are unfortunate symptoms of stylization in the lines of the woman's body, but for a rather late Utamaro the print has much warmth and feeling. It was probably made around 1798.

Plates 26 & 27

RYOGOKU BRIDGE, ABOVE AND BELOW

Six color prints joined. Tokyo National Museum.

Utamaro is best known for his portraits of individual women, but his flair for composition is more strikingly illustrated in group pictures such as the large-scale composite print shown here. Each of the six panels that make up this scene might be viewed separately without seeming incomplete, but balance and unity are remarkably well preserved when they are assembled together. This is partially due to the artist's effective use of the bridge, but the placement of the human beings, though ostensibly lax, plays an important part. The collection of elongated beauties brings to mind similarly conceived prints by Kiyonaga, but at the same time the qualities that distinguish Utamaro from that artist are immediately visible. The easy rhythm that marks this work is foreign to Kiyonaga's style. Somehow Kiyonaga was neater and more proper, but by the same token less in tune with the easy-going spirit of Edo townspeople.

Some critics are of the opinion that there were originally ten sections in this picture, but no others have ever come to light, and it seems needless to suppose that the work is not complete as it stands.

Plate 27. *Section of Plate 26.*

Plate 26

Plate 28

WOMAN READING A LETTER BY LAMPLIGHT

Color Print. Collection of Mr. Shozaburo Watanabe.

A number of ukiyo-e artists, including Masanobu, Harunobu, and Kiyonaga, designed prints in which a woman is shown through a green mosquito net. The thin obstruction lends a soft, remote quality to the subject's physical beauty. Few prints exist in which the net is so prominent or effective as in the example shown here. Unfortunately, in reproduction much is lost because the thin strands of the net are blurred. In the original from which this was taken they are perfectly clear—a marvel of engraving, in fact— and the artist's purpose is completely apparent.

One will observe that the body contours of this woman are more realistic than is often the case with Utamaro. She is not terribly tall, and she has at least substantial weight. The missive in which she is so absorbed is no doubt from her lover.

The handling of light is somewhat obscure. The distinct rays are understandable, but one wonders why the lighted portions of the net seem on the whole darker than the unlighted parts. There is little reason to quibble. The artist was simply more interested in design than in scientific detail.

The series to which this print belongs includes in addition pictures of a weaver, a toothpick-maker, a writing teacher, a laundress, and other working women. Despite the title, the emphasis is on the women themselves rather than on their work, but this is what one would expect from Utamaro. Apparently pictures of this genre were rather popular in the artist's day, since he also produced works entitled *Women Engaged in Making Silk, Various Types of Working Women,* and *Mirror of Women at Work.*

To judge from the degree of stylization in this particular series, one would suppose that it dates from around 1800. This print fortunately is somewhat freer than the others, and the pose of the hairdresser herself is very real and forceful. The colors are subdued and tasteful.

OKITA OF THE NANIWAYA

Color print on both sides of paper. Approximately 13 × 5½ inches. Collection of Mr. Takaharu Mitsui.

Okita was a waitress of considerable fame who worked in the Naniwaya, a teahouse near the temple of Kannon in Asakusa. Shown here gliding by with a teacup and a tobacco tray, she is a study in poise and graceful carriage—those qualities that were so necessary to the successful courtesans of her time.

The picture is not two but one, Okita fore appearing on one side of the paper and Okita aft on the other. As the reader will observe, the contours of the two sides coincide. Perhaps the artist was striving for three-dimensional reality, or perhaps he was merely trying to please both the people who admired Okita's face and those who preferred the gentle curve of her back. In either case, the printing is technically superb. Utamaro also made a picture of the same sort showing Takashima Ohisa, another famous beauty of the time.

This work was probably published in 1791 or 1792.

Plate 30   *Plate 31*

Plate 32

OVERNIGHT GUESTS

Three color prints joined. Collection of Mr. Sei-ichiro Takahashi.

This is the most famous and also the rarest of Utamaro's triptychs. It illustrates a penchant mentioned before for veiling beautiful women with a green mosquito net. The color effect is strange and lovely, and in this case the net serves to unify the three separate sections. In each print a tall woman standing outside the net is balanced against a seated woman inside. The thin barrier provides a sense of depth as well as tonal contrast. The women who have already retired have thrown themselves into the lazy positions that Utamaro portrayed so successfully. Though ostensibly haphazard, this is one of the artist's most careful designs. It alone would place him among the most able of the ukiyo-e designers.

In 1790 Utamaro began an album named *Ten Physiognomical Studies of Women*, but failed to complete it (see Plate 14). Some time between 1801 and 1803, however, he took up the idea again, and the result was the series from which this print is taken. This time he made all ten pictures, but unhappily he was no longer the artist he had been, and few of them are up to the earlier prints. Still, this picture of a girl at work with a millstone is very engaging. The composition is tight, and the youthful face is charming. Utamaro wrote on the print that "this face is very gentle by nature, and the girl is exceptionally steadfast in all her work."

Plate 34

A GOOD-FOR-NOTHING

From "Through the Glasses of a Counseling Parent." Color print. Collection of Mr. Sei-ichiro Takahashi.

The album from which this illustration is taken shows a number of young women calculated to make an upright parent sigh in despair. They include aside from this slovenly creature a "fast woman," a "tipsy woman," a "low-down woman," a "loose woman," and a "whimsical woman." Not very virtuous types, but on the whole lively. The album was made around 1802, and it furnishes a happy contrast to the many stiff, lifeless pictures that Utamaro turned out in this period. The woman has been brushing her teeth, and she is leaning over to spit out a mouthful of water. Due to her position the composition is rather unstable, but it is vivid, and the puffed cheeks and mouth are exceedingly realistic. The writing states what the woman ought to be, as opposed to what she is. The moralizing is perhaps a natural touch for a man of more than fifty, but the lengthy passage rather spoils the artistic effect of the print.

The woman's face, resting against her incredibly delicate
hand, wears an expression of dreamy rapture. Lost in
thoughts of her lover, she is one of Utamaro's most beautiful visions of passionate, tender womanhood. The print
forms a pair with "Love Requited" (Plate 16), for the two
women shown are the oldest of Utamaro's beauties. The
artist seems to have clearly understood the feelings of
women no longer youthful. Here he has managed to
convey not only the physical beauty, but the ageless
femininity of a mature woman in love. See Plate 8 for
detail.

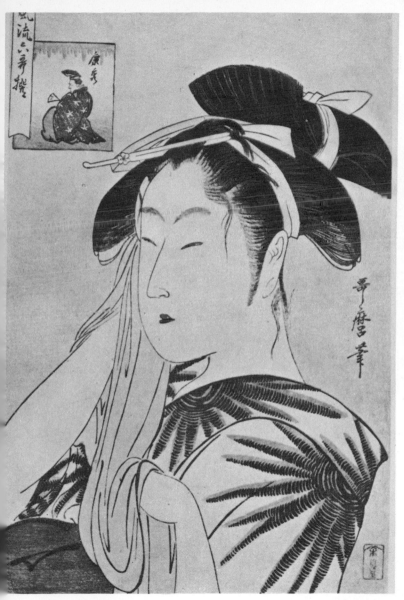

Plate 35. YASUHIDE.
From "Six Elegant Poets." Color print. 1795 or 1796.

Plate 36. TAKASHIMA OHISA.
Color print. 1795 or 1796.

Plate 37. OKITA AT SIXTEEN.
Color print. 1795 or 1796.

Plate 38. A GROUP OF SHELL COLLECTORS.
Color print. 1789.

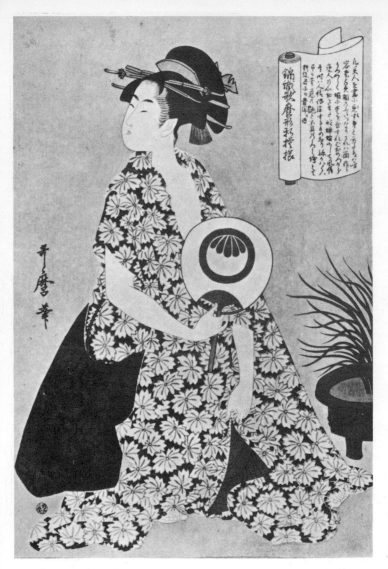

Plate 39. From "New Brocade Design in the Utamaro Style."
Color print. 1794 or 1795.

Plate 40. WOMAN DRINKING FROM A GLASS.
From "Eight Famous Teahouses." Color print. 1795 or 1796.

Plate 41. SHAVING THE BABY'S HEAD.
Color print. 1799 or 1800.

Plate 42. Bathing the Baby.
Color print. 1797 or 1798.

Plates 43, 44 & 45.
HIDEYOSHI AMUSING HIMSELF WITH HIS FIVE CONCUBINES.
Set of three color prints. 1804.

Plate 44. See preceding plate.

Plate 45. *See preceding plate.*

Plate 46. PORTRAIT OF UTAMARO.
By Chobunsai Eishi. 1815. British Museum.

BIOGRAPHICAL CHRONOLOGY

1753 Born.

1775 Entered the school of Toriyama Sekien and took the name
      Kitagawa Hosho. Earliest known album published.

1776 Drew narrow-size pictures of actors. Came under the influence
      of Katsukawa Shunsho.

1781 Changed name to Utamaro.

Plate 47. CHUSHINGURA. *Illustrated text of a play. 1777.*

1782   Painted medium-size pictures of beautiful women.

1784   Moved to the house of Tsutaya Juzaburo. From about this time showed the influence of Kiyonaga. Pupil whose name was recorded around this time as Kitagawa Chiyojo is thought by some to have been his wife, but there is no proof.

1788   Published *A Collection of Insects*, with a comment by Sekien, who died later in the year.

1789   Published "Shiohi no Tsuto" (A Group of Shell Collectors) to which he signed the words *jisei ikka*, or "the independent artist."

1790   Published his last series of illustrations for farcical poetry. Woman closely connected with him (mother, wife, or daughter) died. Began publishing pictures of beautiful women in new style, showing only upper half of the body and using a mica background.

1793   At peak of popularity. In response to requests by many publishers, began to produce at an excessive pace.

1799 Began to put out many pictures based on the story of Kintaro and Yamauba.

1801 Designs took on a distinctly "late-period" look.

1804 Drew "Hideyoshi Amusing Himself with His Five Concubines" and was punished by the government. Placed in prison for a short time and subsequently had hands bound in chains for fifty days.

1806 Died. Buried at Senko-ji, a temple in Setagaya, Tokyo.

BIBLIOGRAPHY

Books on Utamaro in Japanese

Inoue, Kazuo (comp.). *Utamaro Ukiyo-e-shu* (A Collection of Ukiyo-e by Utamaro). 1926.

Odaka, Sennosuke. "Utamaro Ehon-ko" (A Study of Utamaros Picture Albums). In the journal *Ukiyo-e no Kenkyu*, Vol. 20, 1928.

Noguchi, Yonejiro. *Kitagawa Utamaro*. 1931

Kondo, Ichitaro. *Utamaro*. 1941.

Yoshida, Eiji, *Utamaro Zenshu* (The Complete Works of Utamaro). 1941.

Shibui Sei. *Utamaro*. 1952.

Books on Utamaro in Western Languages

Goncourt, E. *Outamaro*. Paris, 1891.

Kurth, J. *Utamaro*. Leipzig, 1907.

General Books on Ukiyo-e

Ficke, A. C. *Chats on Japanese Prints*. London, 1915.

Binyon, L. *Catalogue of Japanese and Chinese Woodcuts in the British Museum*. London, 1916.

Binyon, L. and Sexton, J. J. *Japanese Colour Prints*. London, 1923.

Blunt, W. *Japanese Colour Prints from Harunobu to Utamaro*. London, 1952.

Metropolitan Museum of Art Miniatures. *Japanese Prints in the Metropolitan*. New York, 1952.

Hillier, J. *Japanese Masters of the Colour Print*. London, 1954.

Michener, J. *The Floating World*. New York, 1954.